KT-162-462

BARCELONA

BARCELONA

Photographs by Alejandro Bachrach
Text by Aurora Cuito

teNeues

Para los que disfrutan del sol, el mar, la arena, un chapuzón y la brisa.

Para los que buscan una luz que cambia con las estaciones del año, con las horas del día, y que matiza, resalta o inunda detalles y rincones.

Para los que se maravillan con tiempos pasados, con vestigios de imperios derrotados, con murallas romanas, iglesias románicas y palacios góticos.

Para los que se fascinan con los edificios modernistas, sus mosaicos, las formas orgánicas, las figuras mitológicas, los vitrales, el hierro forjado y los artesonados de madera.

Para los gourmets que saborean la paella, el jamón, el pescado fresco, los dulces y el vino tinto, blanco o espumoso.

Para los que prefieren la vida en la calle, la tertulia en una terraza, un paseo por la playa, un concierto en una plaza o simplemente el deambular por la Rambla.

Para los amantes del arte, de los inicios de Picasso, del surrealismo de Dalí, de la frescura de Miró o de la extravagancia de Tàpies.

Para los que excita el bullicio urbano, la abundancia de actividades propias de una ciudad cosmopolita, las obras de teatro, las exposiciones y la variada oferta comercial.

Pero también para los que buscan un remanso de tranquilidad, una callejuela silenciosa, un parque con vistas al mar o un refugio.

Para los que prefieren el contacto con la gente, el día a día de los habitantes, las costumbres y las actividades cotidianas.

Para los que se enriquecen con los contrastes, el convivir de lo nuevo y lo antiguo, lo permanente y lo anecdótico, lo estético y lo grotesco, la tradición y la modernidad, los monumentos y las realidades más modestas.

Para todos ellos, viajeros, habitantes y curiosos, Barcelona abre sus puertas y ofrece lo mejor de sí misma.

Aurora Cuito

For those who enjoy sunshine, sea, sand, a leap into the water and a gentle breeze.

For those who seek a certain daylight, changing with every season, with each hour of the day, emphasizing, flooding, subtly tracing each detail and outline.

For those who marvel at times gone by, vanished empires with their Roman city walls, romanesque churches and gothic palaces.

For those who are fascinated by art nouveau architecture with its mosaics, organic forms, mythological figures, stained glass windows, wrought ironwork and wooden coffered ceilings.

For gourmets who relish paella, hams, fresh fish, sweet desserts and red, white or sparkling wine.

For those who enjoy the street life, an amicable gathering on the terrace, a walk along the beach, a concert on the plaza or simply a stroll along the Rambla.

For the art lover; the initial works of Picasso, the surrealism of Dalí, the audacity of Miró or the extravagances of Tàpies.

For those who love to plunge into the bustle of urban life, into the vast range of activities which such a cosmopolitan city has to offer: Theater, exhibitions and the variety of commercial offers.

But also for those who seek an oasis of tranquility, a quiet back street, a park with a view across the sea, a refuge.

For those who prefer contact with people and the day to day life of the populace, the customs and the activities of everyday life.

For those enriched by contrast, the convergence of the new with the old, the immutable and the anecdotal, the aesthetic and the grotesque, the traditional and the modern, the monuments and the more modest realities.

For all those, the travelers, the inhabitants and the curious, Barcelona opens its portals and presents its most delightful aspects.

Aurora Cuito

Für die, die sich an Sonne, Meer, Sand, einem Sprung ins Wasser und einer angenehmen Brise erfreuen.

Für die, die ein Licht suchen, das zu jeder Jahreszeit, zu jeder Stunde des Tages anders ist, das Einzelheiten und Konturen nuanciert, hervorhebt, überflutet.

Für die, die vergangenen Zeiten nachspüren, untergegangenen Reichen mit ihren römischen Stadtmauern, romanischen Kirchen und gotischen Palästen.

Für die, die sich für Jugendstil-Architektur begeistern mit ihren Mosaiken, organischen Formen, mythologischen Figuren, den Glasfenstern, dem Schmiedeeisen und den getäfelten Kassettendecken.

Für die Feinschmecker, die die Paella, den Schinken, den frischen Fisch und die Süßspeisen zu genießen wissen – nicht zu vergessen den Wein, ob rot, weiß oder schäumend.

Für die, die gerne im Freien sind, in einer geselligen Runde auf einer Terrasse, beim Spaziergang am Strand, bei einem Konzert auf einem Platz oder die einfach nur über die Rambla schlendern wollen.

Für die Liebhaber der Kunst, der Anfänge Picassos, des Surrealismus Dalís, der Unbekümmertheit Mirós oder der Extravaganz Tàpies'.

Für die, die es lieben, sich in den Trubel des urbanen Lebens zu stürzen, in die Unmenge an Aktivitäten, die eine kosmopolitische Stadt anzubieten hat, die Theater, Ausstellungen und vielfältigen kommerziellen Angebote.

Aber auch für die, die eine Oase der Ruhe suchen, ein stilles Gässchen, einen Park mit Blick aufs Meer, ein Refugium.

Für die, die gerne mit Leuten zusammenkommen und die Einwohner, deren Bräuche und das alltägliche Leben kennenlernen möchten.

Für die, die Gegensätze lieben, das Aufeinandertreffen des Neuen mit dem Alten, des Dauerhaften mit dem Flüchtigen, des Ästhetischen mit dem Grotesken, der Tradition mit der Moderne, der Monumente mit der bescheideneren Wirklichkeit.

Für sie alle, die Reisenden, die Einwohner, die Neugierigen, öffnet Barcelona seine Pforten und zeigt sich von seiner schönsten Seite.

Aurora Cuito

Pour ceux qui goûtent le soleil, la mer, le sable, le plongeon dans l'eau et la caresse d'une brise.

Pour ceux qui sont attirés par la lumière qui change avec chaque saison de l'année et avec chaque heure de la journée, qui réalise des nuances et fait ressortir ou inonde les détails et les recoins.

Pour ceux qui s'émerveillent en retrouvant le passé, les vestiges des murailles romaines qui rappellent des empires disparus, les églises romanes et les palais gothiques.

Pour ceux que fascinent l'architecture de style Art nouveau, ses mosaïques, les formes organiques, les figures mythologiques, les vitraux, le fer forgé et les plafonds pannelés à caissons.

Pour les gourmets qui aiment la paella, le jambon, le poisson frais et les douceurs, mais aussi déguster les vins rouges, blancs ou mousseux.

Pour ceux qui préfèrent vivre dans la rue, être en société sur une terrasse, se promener sur la plage, assister à un concert sur la place ou simplement flâner sur la Rambla.

Pour les amateurs d'art, l'art initial de Picasso, le surréalisme de Dalí, la fraîcheur de Miró ou l'extravagance de Tàpies.

Pour ceux qui s'adonnent à l'excitation que procurent le bouillonnement de la vie urbaine, les nombreuses activités d'une cité cosmopolite, le théâtre, les expositions et la multitude des offres commerciales.

Mais aussi pour ceux qui recherchent une oasis de paix, une ruelle paisible, un parc avec vue sur la mer ou un refuge.

Pour ceux qui préfèrent les contacts et veulent connaître les habitants, leurs coutumes et leur vie quotidienne.

Pour ceux qui se passionnent pour les contrastes, pour la coexistence du nouveau et de l'ancien, pour le permanent et l'anecdotique, l'esthétique et le grotesque, les traditions et le modernisme, les monuments et la réalité plus modeste.

Pour tous ceux-là, qu'ils soient voyageurs, habitants ou curieux, Barcelone ouvre ses portes et leur offre tout ce qu'elle a de mieux.

Aurora Cuito

A chi ama il sole, il mare, la spiaggia, un tuffo in acqua, la brezza.

A chi è in cerca di una luce che muti con le stagioni e le ore del giorno, una luce che faccia risaltare le sfumature, che scolpisca e inondi dettagli e scorci.

A chi ama le meraviglie di epoche passate, le vestigia di imperi decaduti, le mura romane, le chiese romaniche, i palazzi gotici.

A chi è sensibile al fascino dell'architettura liberty, ai suoi mosaici, all'organicità delle forme, alle figure mitologiche, alle vetrate, ai lavori in ferro battuto e ai soffitti a cassettoni di legno.

Ai buongustai con la passione della paella, del buon prosciutto, del pesce fresco, dei dolci e del vino rosso, bianco o spumante.

A chi predilige la vita all'aperto, la convivialità da terrazza, le passeggiate in spiaggia, i concerti di piazza o anche solo bighellonare per la Rambla.

A chi ama l'arte, il primo Picasso, il surrealismo di Dalí, la freschezza di Miró e la stravaganza di Tápies.

A chi si esalta per il ribollire della città, le incessanti attività di una metropoli cosmopolita, gli allestimenti teatrali, le mostre e l'enorme offerta commerciale.

Ma anche a chi è in cerca di un'oasi tranquilla, del vicoletto silenzioso, del giardino con vista sul mare, di un rifugio.

A chi preferisce il contatto con la gente, la quotidianità della popolazione locale, gli usi e le attività di tutti i giorni.

A chi si sente arricchito dai contrasti, dalla convivenza tra nuovo e antico, eterno ed aneddotico, bello e grottesco, tradizione e modernità, monumenti e realtà più modeste.

A tutti loro, viaggiatori, residenti e curiosi, Barcellona apre le sue porte offrendo il meglio di sé.

Aurora Cuito

Directorio   Directory   Verzeichnis   Table des matières   Indice delle materie

Front cover: Passeig de Gràcia, Casa Batlló
© Casa Batlló, S.L.
Back cover: Tibidabo, Plaça de Dr. Andreu

Photographs © 2003 Alejandro Bachrach
© 2003 teNeues Verlag GmbH + Co. KG, Kempen
All rights reserved.

Alejandro Bachrach
Josep Rodoreda 35, entresuelo 1
Esplugues de Llobregat
08950 Barcelona, España
Phone: 0034-93-47 38 296
Fax: 0034-93-47 36 214
Mobile: 0034-62 02 59 167
www.alebachrach.com
info@alebachrach.com

Photographs by Alejandro Bachrach, Barcelona
Design by Anika Leppkes
Introduction by Aurora Cuito
Translation by Werkstatt München – Martin Waller
Jon Smale (English)
Martin Waller (German)
Nathalie Kouznetzoff (French)
Marco Montemarano (Italian)
Editorial coordination by Sabine Wagner
Production by Sandra Jansen
Color separation by Medien Team-Vreden, Germany

While we strive for utmost precision in every detail,
we cannot be held responsible for any inaccuracies,
neither for any subsequent loss or damage arising.

Bibliographic information published by Die Deutsche
Bibliothek. Die Deutsche Bibliothek lists this publica-
tion in the Deutsche Nationalbibliografie; detailed
bibliographic data is available in the Internet at
http://dnb.ddb.de

ISBN 3-8238-4550-0

Printed in Italy

Published by teNeues Publishing Group

teNeues Book Division
Kaistraße 18
40221 Düsseldorf
Germany
Phone: 00 49-(0)2 11-99 45 97-0
Fax: 00 49-(0)2 11-99 45 97-40
e-mail: books@teneues.de
Press department: arehn@teneues.de
Phone: 00 49-(0) 21 52-916-202

teNeues Publishing Company
16 West 22nd Street
New York, N.Y. 10010
USA
Phone: 001-212-627-9090
Fax: 001-212-627-9511

teNeues Publishing UK Ltd.
P. O. Box 402
West Byfleet
KT14 7ZF
Great Britain
Phone: 0044-1932-403509
Fax: 0044-1932-403514

teNeues France S.A.R.L.
4, rue de Valence
75005 Paris
France
Phone: 00 33-1-55 76 62 05
Fax: 00 33-1-55 76 64 19

www.teneues.com

teNeues Publishing Group
Kempen
Düsseldorf
London
Madrid
New York
Paris

teNeues